Color Your Way to a Life You Love™

FORGIVE YOURSELF

A SELF-HELP ADULT COLORING BOOK FOR RELAXATION & PERSONAL GROWTH!

60 CALMING DESIGNS TO COLOR!
FLOWERS & NATURE
ANIMALS
MANDALAS
DOODLES & PATTERNS

COLOR YOUR WAY TO A LIFE YOU LOVE™: FORGIVE YOURSELF

For information:
shellijohnson.com
alphadollmedia.com

Copyright Notice and Disclaimers

This book is Copyright © 2017 Shelli Johnson (the "Author"). All Rights Reserved. Published in the United States of America. The legal notices, disclosures, and disclaimers within this book are copyrighted by the Internet Attorneys Association LLC and licensed for use by the Author in this book. All rights reserved.

No part of this book may be reproduced or transmitted in any form or by any means, electronic or mechanical, including photocopying, recording, or by an information storage and retrieval system -- except by a reviewer who may quote brief passages in a review to be printed in a magazine, newspaper, blog, or website -- without permission in writing from the Author. For information, please contact the Author at the following website address: shellijohnson.com/contact

For more information, please read the "Disclosures and Disclaimers" section at the end of this book.

First Paperback Print Edition, November 2017

Published by Alpha Doll Media, LLC (the "Publisher").

ISBN: 978-0-9747109-5-2

WELCOME TO THE
COLOR YOUR WAY TO A LIFE YOU LOVE™
COLORING BOOK SERIES!

 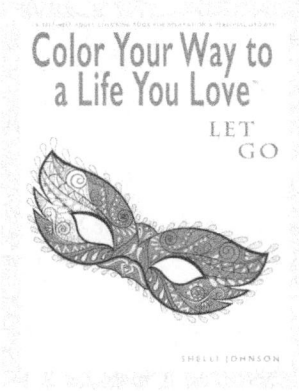 

AVAILABLE NOW OR COMING SOON!

UNLEASH YOUR INNER CREATOR & MAKE IT YOUR OWN!

This is not just another coloring book, it's also an invitation for you to delve deeper into who you are so you can find out what makes you come alive. I'm a big believer in the power of taking small steps to get you anywhere you need or want to go. With that in mind, I invite you inside these pages on a creative self-help adventure. You'll unleash your artistic side with designs and patterns while you do daily small-sized activities aimed at: 1. helping you heal yourself and 2. inspiring you to create a life you love. My hope is that you'll use these pages to ignite your imagination, discard your limitations, and free your inner creator.

Feel free to add your own personal embellishments to any image. You can make each page as unique as you like by adding doodles, patterns, and/or shapes. Color the images any way you like with any tools you like. There are no rules except that you relax, enjoy, and color in a way that feels right to you.

THE MEANING & PURPOSE OF LIFE!

"The meaning of life is to find your gift.
The purpose of life is to give it away."
—Pablo Picasso

THE PSYCHOLOGY OF COLOR!

From my layman's understanding of the meaning of colors, certain colors can evoke certain emotions.

BLUE: centered, calm, hopeful, confidence
GREEN: growth, safety, endurance, calm
ORANGE: energy, happiness, encouragement, excitement
RED: passion, energy, strength, power, determination
YELLOW: joy, energy, cheerfulness
BROWN: stability
PURPLE: power, ambition, creativity, energy
BLACK: power, elegance, mystery
WHITE: light, goodness, safety

So keep that in mind as you color. If you're looking to experience a particular emotion/feeling/mood, you may want to use a particular color to help you get there.

A FEW HELPFUL SUGGESTIONS!

BABY STEPS
I'm a big believer in the power of taking baby steps to get you anywhere you need or want to go, which is why this coloring book is written the way it is. Each day has small-sized activities. They build on each other, one to the next. So feel free to color whichever image you'd like, just know you'll be best served to do the daily activities in order.

NO PERFECTION NEEDED
Do yourself a kindness and make a mistake in this coloring book early on. Scribble on some of the pages. Spill your favorite beverage on the cover. Rip one of the corners off. Color outside the lines. Make this book imperfect so that you'll feel free to be your real, honest self inside the pages. Being real, not being perfect, is what's going to heal you and set you free.

BE HONEST
I'd recommend that you don't show your answers inside this coloring book to anyone. Keep them to yourself for right now until you make it all the way through Day 30. Why? Honesty with yourself is what's going to help you heal and grow. You won't be completely honest if you're worried about someone reading your answers. In fact, what you're likely to do is tweak your responses, edit them, or scratch them out entirely if you're worried about how others might perceive you. So be kind to yourself & let this coloring book be just for you.

BE WILLING & OPEN
The first step to change is to be open & willing to it. You picked up this coloring book because you're struggling in this area of your life. If you want things to be different, well, both you & those things are going to have to change. So be open to experiencing something new & be willing to do the effort to get there.

GIVE YOURSELF PERMISSION
It's hugely important to give yourself permission (whether that's verbally or written) to: do the daily steps in this book, be/have/do/say/believe whatever you need to so that you can heal yourself, give yourself unlimited tries as many times as it takes, believe in your own worth and value, choose to create a life you love because you matter. Whenever you feel like you need someone else's permission to make a choice about your life, you just give that permission to yourself. The only permission you ever need to live your own life is your own.

YOU'RE ON A JOURNEY
It doesn't matter how old you are, how many times you've tried, or how far there is left to go. It's never too late to be the person you want to be. It's okay if you don't know things yet. You're on a journey and you'll figure it out as you go. This coloring book is designed to help you do just that.

BEGIN YOUR DAY WITH A STEP
If at all possible, do your daily step shortly after you wake up. That way, you'll be able to focus on yourself (because you're absolutely worth the time to do that) before your day gets away from you. So grab your favorite beverage. Find a quiet place. Relax and reflect while you're being creative.

IT'S A PRACTICE & A PROCESS
There's no doing this perfectly, and that's okay. You strive for progress. You do the best you can. So show yourself some patience and kindness because self-compassion is what you most need to heal yourself. You will make mistakes, there's just no way around it. Don't ever use any mistake as a reason to give up on yourself. Just circle back around and start again. And know this: every mistake is simply a brand new chance to do it better the next time.

AND FINALLY...
Remember (not just for this book but for all of life): you get out what you put in. So make yourself a priority in your own life because: 1. you're absolutely worth the effort and 2. no one else can do it for you. And one last suggestion good both for this book and for all of life: be brave and color outside the lines, that's where freedom lies.

THOSE WHO ARE BRAVE ARE FREE!

"It is not the critic who counts; not the man who points out how the strong man stumbles, or where the doer of deeds could have done them better. The credit belongs to the man who is actually in the arena, whose face is marred by dust and sweat and blood; who strives valiantly; who errs, who comes short again and again, because there is no effort without error and shortcoming; but who does actually strive to do the deeds; who knows great enthusiasms, the great devotions; who spends himself in a worthy cause; who at the best knows in the end the triumph of high achievement, and who at the worst, if he fails, at least fails while daring greatly, so that his place shall never be with those cold and timid souls who neither know victory nor defeat."

—Theodore Roosevelt

Source: excerpt (also known as *The Man In The Arena*) from the speech "Citizenship in a Republic" delivered at The Sorbonne in Paris, France on April 23, 1910.

COLOR TEST PAGE

You got to love yourself enough to forgive yourself,
over and over and over again, many times as it takes.
A hundred. A thousand. A million. Don't matter.
You got to love yourself enough to give yourself unlimited
chances too, many times as it takes. You got to love yourself
enough 'cause that's the only way you're ever gonna find peace.
—Ned Horner

1

1. Today, relax.
2. Take a deep breath in through your nose.
3. Hold it for three seconds.
4. Let it out through your mouth.
5. Then pull your shoulders down away from your ears.
6. Repeat five times.
7. Massage your temples & the back of your neck.
8. Repeat often, especially every time you feel a lack of self-forgiveness &/or a lack of self-compassion.

2.

1. Today, know that you are not alone.
2. You may feel alone. You may feel like everyone else is moving on while you struggle to forgive yourself for the things you did or failed to do.
3. But know this: it's not just you. I have been there. So have most, if not all, of the people around you.
4. So don't be so hard on yourself.
5. Remind yourself that you're not alone, that you are in fact in excellent company with the rest of us, as often as needed.

3

1. Today, practice self-compassion.
2. Know this: compassion is what you feel when you see someone else struggling/suffering & your heart breaks for them so you want to help.
3. Self-compassion is turning that same feeling of tenderness/kindness & wanting to help ease the struggling/suffering toward yourself.
4. Always remember: self-compassion is what you most need to heal yourself & bring yourself peace.
5. So practice self-compassion all day. If you are unkind to you, *gently* tell yourself to stop. Be patient & just start being kind to you again.

4

1. Today, check your motivation.
2. Know this: you won't fully heal if your motivation for forgiving yourself is because others say you should. *You* need to choose to do it *for you*.
3. Write the answer to this: *Why do I want to forgive myself?*
4. If the answer has anything to do with someone else, then you're not your sole motivation.
5. Choose to forgive yourself not for what you might gain from others but for what you'll gain for yourself.

Practice self-compassion. Be kind to you all day.

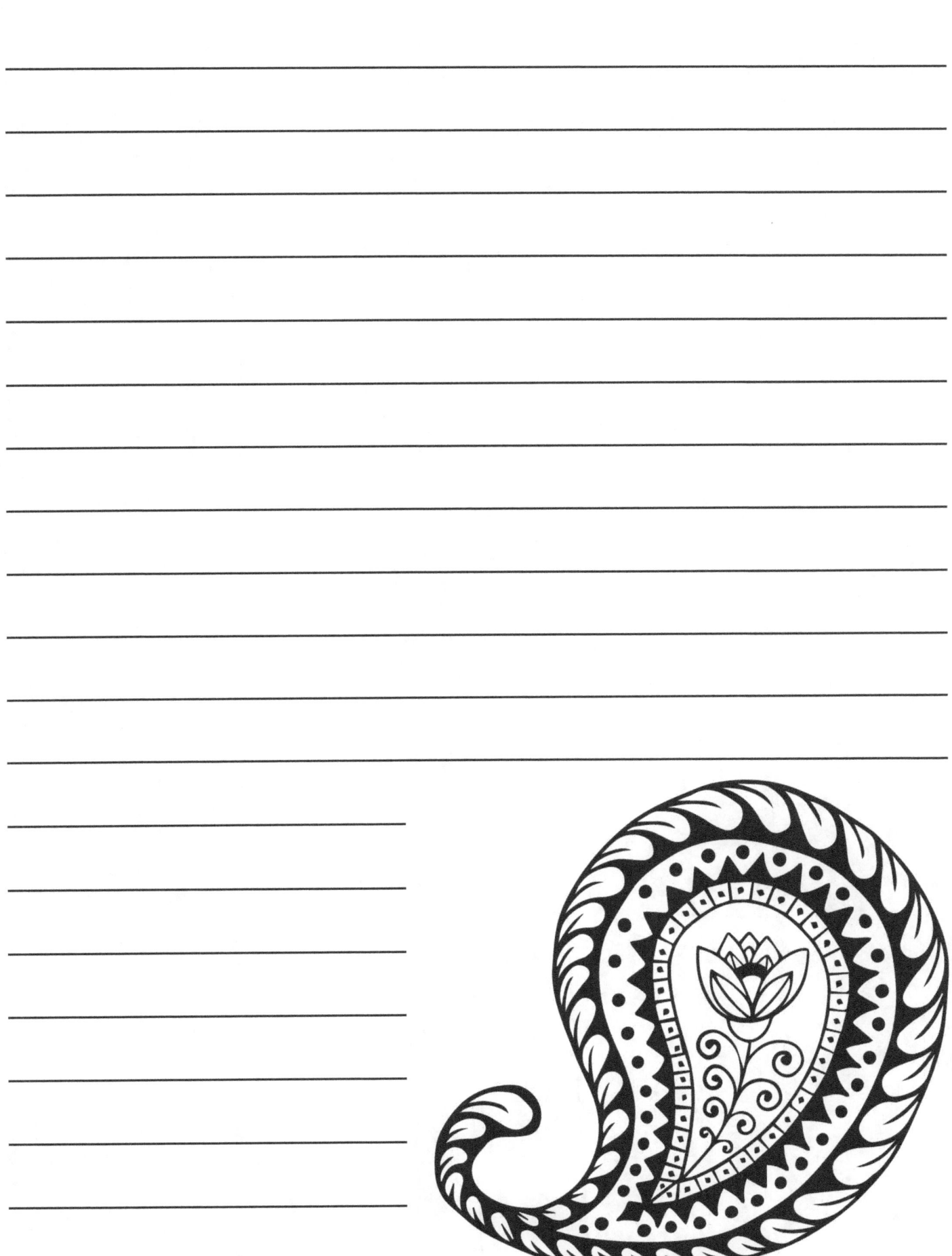

5

1. Today, commit to your own healing.
2. Resolve that you want to be healthy & whole (emotionally, physically, mentally, & spiritually).
3. Be willing *daily* to take whatever action you need to heal yourself.
4. So take the escape clause out of your commitment. Write (yes, write it down) an unbreakable promise to yourself that no matter what happens or how challenging it may get, you won't turn on yourself. Instead, you'll see your healing through to the end, until you are healthy & whole.

Practice self-compassion. Be kind to you all day.

6

1. Today, give yourself permission to forgive yourself.
2. Know this: you don't need others to forgive you in order to forgive yourself. You don't need anyone else's permission either. The only permission you ever need for self-forgiveness is your own.
3. So write yourself a permission slip.
4. Write a note that says you're allowed & need to forgive yourself for whatever it was you did or failed to do.
5. Believe that note & refer back to it as needed.

Practice self-compassion. Be kind to you all day.

7

1. Today, believe you are forgiven.
2. Look yourself in the eyes in a mirror.
3. Say aloud: *I forgive you*.
4. Say aloud: *I am forgiven*.
5. Repeat *daily & often* until the fact that you forgive yourself & you are forgiven becomes part of the story that you believe about your life.

Practice self-compassion. Be kind to you all day.

8

1. Today, come alive.
2. Write the answers to these: *What do I love to do &/or what lights a spark in me? What activities make me feel the most alive? What are my gifts & talents & passions (things that I love & enjoy)?*
3. Write the first responses that pop into your head. Don't judge or edit.
4. Now pick one item (or more!) from that list & go do it today.
5. Let loose for a little while. Take your mind off everything.
6. Have fun & relax.

Be kind to you. Look in a mirror & say aloud: I forgive you. I am forgiven.

9

1. Today, take an honest inventory of your unforgiveness.
2. Write a list of events/mistakes/failures/happenings/etcetera from your past that you refuse to forgive yourself for.
3. Get still & quiet. Then add anything else that comes up onto your list.
4. Lay out everything you're holding over your own head so you can see it all in one place.
5. Then take a deep breath in through your nose, hold three seconds, let it out your mouth.

Be kind to you. Look in a mirror & say aloud: I forgive you. I am forgiven.

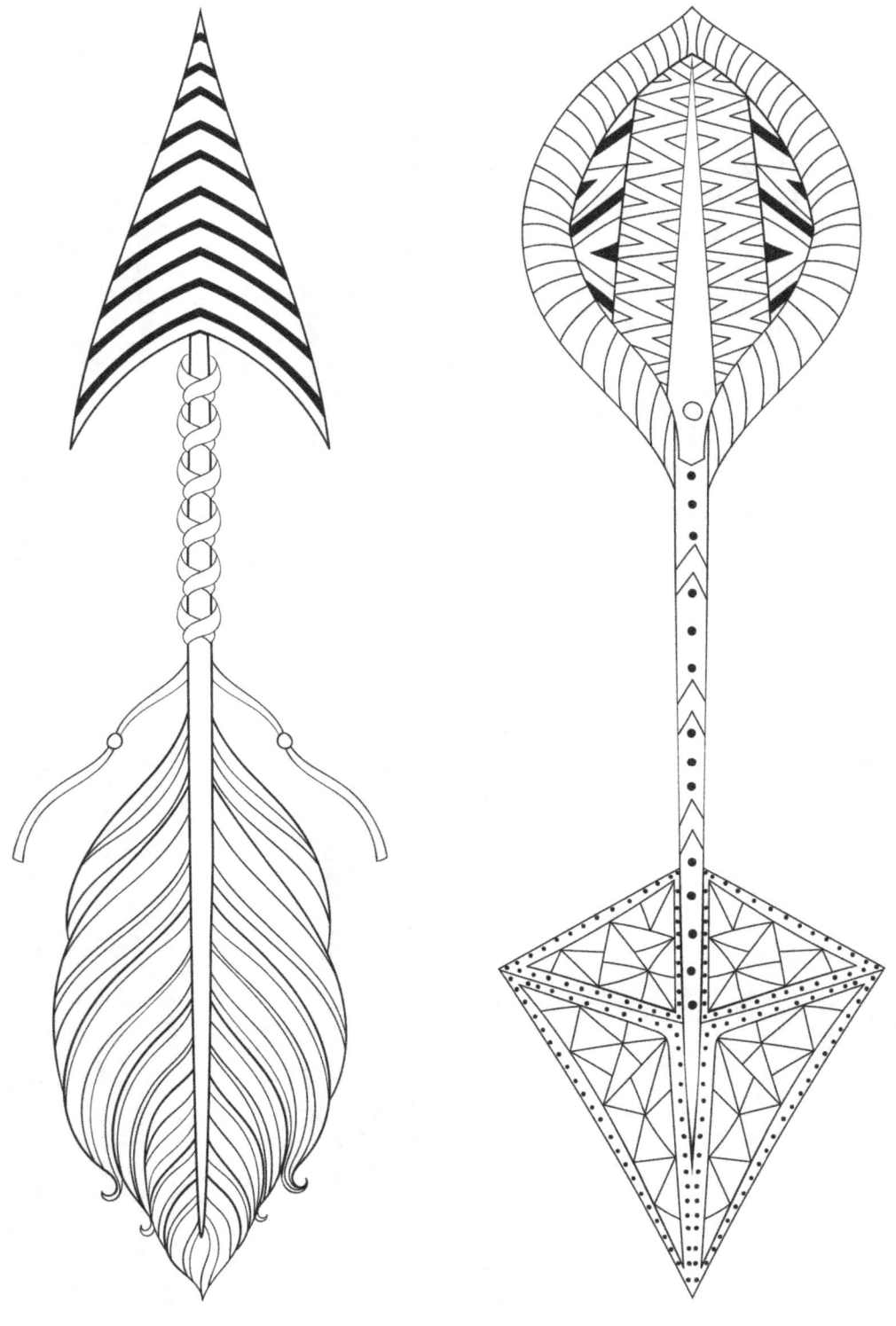

10

1. Today, save your own life.
2. Take full responsibility for your own happiness.
3. Know this: your life doesn't belong to anybody but you. You are responsible for your own happiness. Remember that *every time* you make a choice.
4. Now write the answer to this: *Is not forgiving myself making me joyful & increasing my happiness?*
5. Then write what would bring you joy/happiness. Choose that instead.

*Be kind to you. Look in a mirror & say aloud: *I forgive you. I am forgiven.**

11

1. Today, befriend yourself.
2. Know this: you are with you 24/7. You are the closest & best friend you'll ever have. Refusing to forgive yourself is not being a friend to yourself, it's not having your own back; rather, it's an act of self-abuse.
3. So resolve today not to turn on yourself. No beating yourself up, *ever*.
4. Instead, choose to treat yourself with kindness & respect *every day*, just like a good friend would.
5. Now look at your list from Day 8. Pick one & do it today.

*Be kind to you. Look in a mirror & say aloud: *I forgive you. I am forgiven.**

12

1. Today, examine your history.
2. Read through your list from Day 9.
3. For each item on your list, write answers to these: *Is not forgiving myself changing the past? Is it making what I did or failed to do different in any way?*
4. Take a deep breath in through your nose, hold three seconds, let it out your mouth. Repeat often.
5. Know this: you hold on to your history at the expense of your present & your future.

***Be kind to you. Look in a mirror & say aloud:** I forgive you. I am forgiven.*

13

1. Today, discover the why.
2. Read though your list from Day 9.
3. Next to each one write down why you refuse to forgive yourself.
4. For each one, write the answer to this: *How is not forgiving myself about this serving me?*
5. Know this: you're getting some benefit from not forgiving yourself, I say gently, or else you'd stop doing it. Perhaps it's a habit, a distraction, fear of moving forward/letting go, etcetera. Find out what it is for you.

*Be kind to you. Look in a mirror & say aloud: *I forgive you. I am forgiven.**

14

1. Today, look at your history in a different light.
2. Read your list from Day 9.
3. For each one, write the answers to these: *Is it possible I just made a mistake? Or made a decision out of fear/anger/sadness/loneliness/arrogance/etcetera? Or maybe I was young & naive? Or maybe, no matter my age, I simply didn't know better & so I didn't do better?*
4. Take a deep breath in through your nose, hold three seconds, let it out your mouth. Repeat often.

*Be kind to you. Look in a mirror & say aloud: *I forgive you. I am forgiven.******

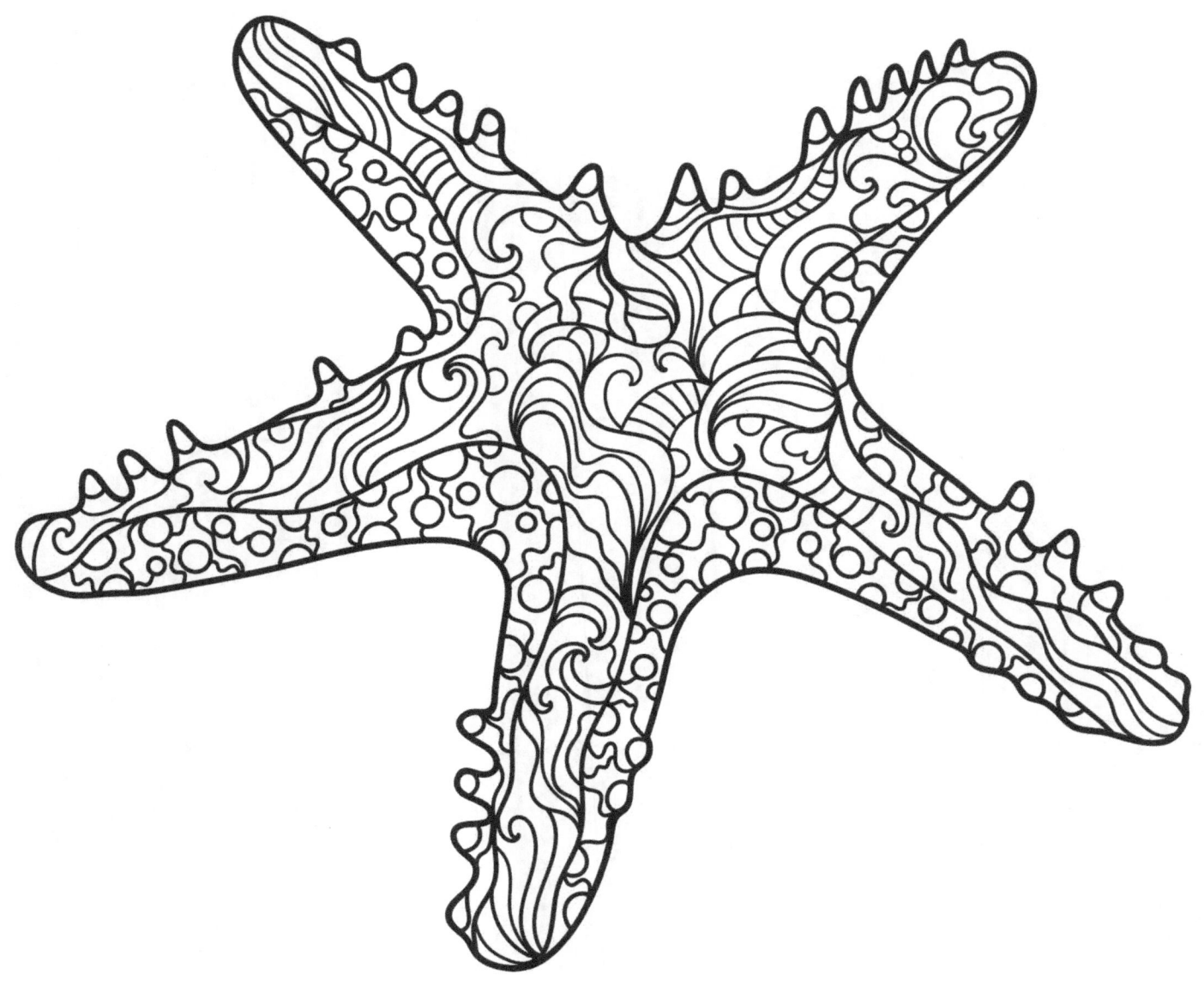

15

1. Today, learn from your history.
2. Read through your list from Day 9.
3. For each item on your list, write the answer to this: *What can I learn about my behavior/choices/motivation from what I did or failed to do?*
4. Now learn what you can & apply it moving forward.
5. Know this: every mistake/failure is simply a brand new chance to try again from a more intelligent perspective. Every mistake/failure is simply a brand new chance to do it better the next time.

*Be kind to you. Look in a mirror & say aloud: *I forgive you. I am forgiven.**

16

1. Today, learn from your history some more.
2. Read through your list from Day 9.
3. For each item on your list, write the answer to this: *What was this meant to teach me about my character/personality?*
4. Be open to the answers that come. Maybe those events/mistakes/failures/happenings/etcetera were there to teach you how strong/tenacious/generous/lenient/persevering/etcetera that you truly are. Maybe they were there to teach you about who you most want to become.

*Be kind to you. Look in a mirror & say aloud: *I forgive you. I am forgiven.**

17

1. Today, befriend yourself again.
2. Read your answers from Day 16 like you're your own best friend.
3. For each item, write your answer to this: *What kind/supportive/nurturing thing do I most need to hear right now?*
4. Then read your answers aloud like you'd want your best friend to talk to you. Use terms of endearment like: *babe, honey, sweet pea, darlin.*
5. Find a mirror, look yourself in the eyes, & say it to yourself.
6. Repeat often, especially whenever you need a kind word.

*Be kind to you. Look in a mirror & say aloud: *I forgive you. I am forgiven.******

18

1. Today, be willing.
2. Write your current age. Now read through your list from Day 9. For each item, write the age you were when that particular item occurred.
3. Subtract. That's how much time you've been imprisoned in unforgiveness.
4. Take a deep breath in through your nose, hold three seconds, let it out your mouth. Repeat often.
5. Now be willing to free yourself today.

*Be kind to you. Look in a mirror & say aloud: *I forgive you. I am forgiven.******

19

1. Today, free yourself.
2. Choose to see not forgiving yourself as an anchor, holding you fixed to a spot, keeping you stuck there.
3. Know this: self-forgiveness is simply a letting go.
4. It doesn't have to be emotionally charged. You can just choose to stop hanging on to whatever you did or failed to do so you can move forward without it.
5. Make forgiving yourself about saving your own life.

*Be kind to you. Look in a mirror & say aloud: *I forgive you. I am forgiven.**

20

1. Today, live in the present moment.
2. Know this: the past will teach you & the future will give you goals if you let them. But the only place you can change anything is in the present.
3. Take a deep breath in through your nose, hold three seconds, let it out your mouth. Repeat often.
4. Now look at your list from Day 8.
5. Pick one & do it today.

Be kind to you. Look in a mirror & say aloud: *I forgive you. I am forgiven.*

21

1. Today, be open to change.
2. Know this: the first step to accepting change is to be open to it.
3. Read through your lists from Days 9 & 13. Then write the story you are telling yourself about your history. (*This/that was my fault because; I should have; if only I could be; if only I hadn't, etcetera.*)
4. Now be open to the possibility of changing that story & viewing your history in a new light. Be willing to believe something new.

*Be kind to you. Look in a mirror & say aloud: *I forgive you. I am forgiven.**

22

1. Today, let go of your history.
2. Read through your list from Day 9.
3. For each item on your list, write the answer to this: *What do I need to do to let this go (make amends, apologize, fix what is fixable, change your choices/ behavior/motivation/character, deal with the consequences, perform a small ceremony, write a note to the person you hurt, etcetera)?*
4. Pick one action you need to do so you can let go. Do it today. Repeat until you've let go of all the history that's keeping you anchored.

*Be kind to you. Look in a mirror & say aloud: *I forgive you. I am forgiven.******

23

1. Today, change the story you tell yourself.
2. Read through the lists you wrote on Days 14, 15, & 16.
3. Using those lists as guides, change the story you tell yourself about your history & what you did or failed to do.
4. Write a new story, one that is true & also self-compassionate.
5. Let that new story be what you tell about yourself & what you choose to believe about your life from now on.

*Be kind to you. Look in a mirror & say aloud: *I forgive you. I am forgiven.******

24

1. Today, aim for progress & not perfection.
2. See yourself as the imperfect human being that you are.
3. Know this: there's no doing life without mistakes/failures; you're in excellent company with the rest of us just trying to figure it out.
4. So cut yourself some slack. Take a deep breath in through your nose, hold three seconds, let it out your mouth. Repeat often.
5. Write down the progress you've made so far & be proud of yourself.
6. Then go do something nice for you.

Be kind to you. Look in a mirror & say aloud: I forgive you. I am forgiven.

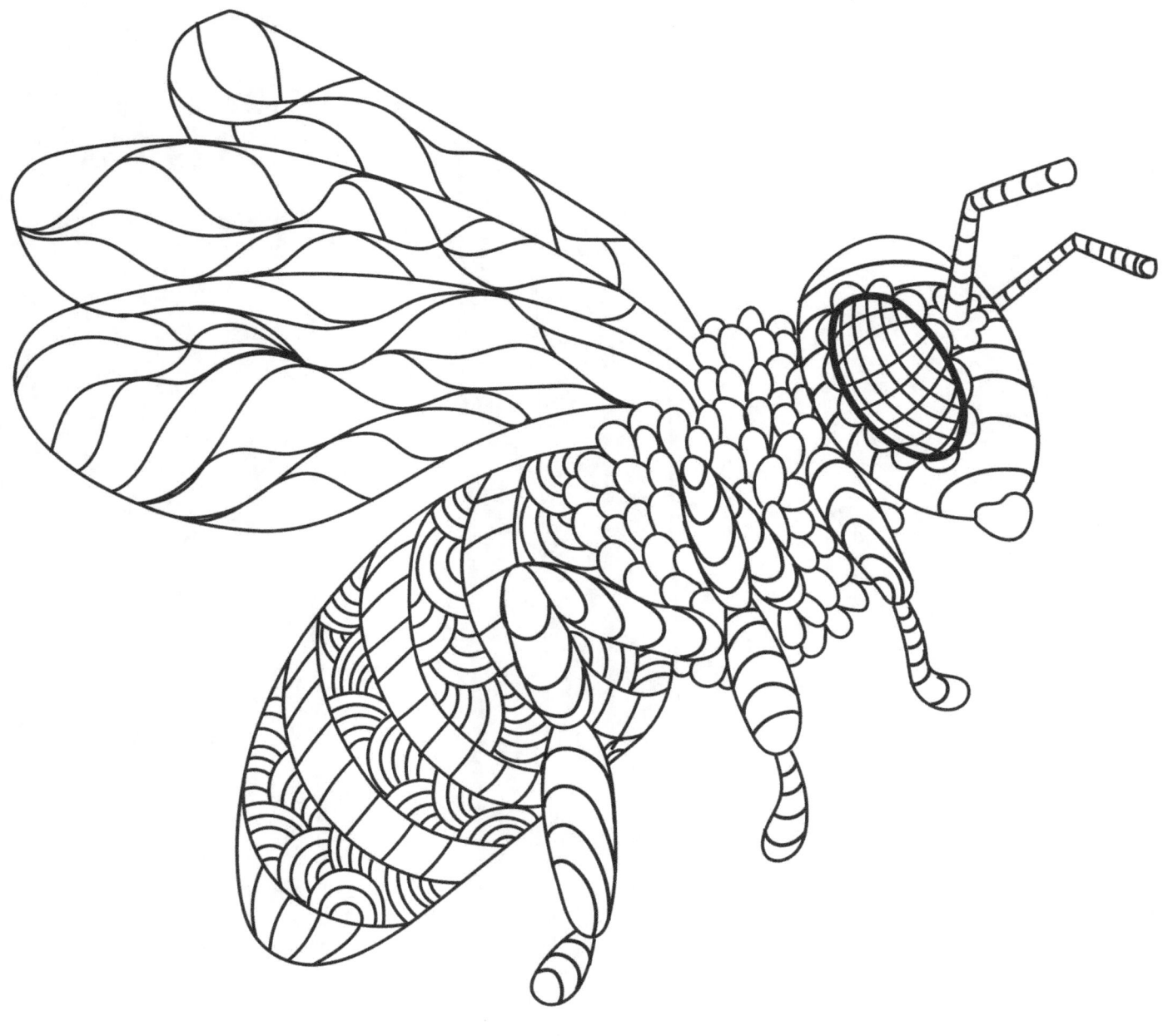

25

1. Today, move on.
2. You have examined your history. You have fixed what you can & learned from what you can't. You have changed the story you tell yourself & let go of your past. That's all you can do & that's enough.
3. Now move forward from a more informed & intelligent perspective.
4. Remember: every mistake is simply a brand new chance to do it better the next time.
5. Now look at your list from Day 8. Pick one & do it today.

Be kind to you. Look in a mirror & say aloud: I forgive you. I am forgiven.

26

1. Today, practice hopefulness.
2. Know this: self-forgiveness is filled with hope.
3. So look for what's hopeful in whatever situation you're going through. Even if there's only a sliver, a tiny glimmer. Even if it takes some serious excavating to find. Look hard. Keep looking until you find it.
4. Write a list of what is good in your life. Then write a list of what good you hope will come out of whatever you're going through.
5. Hang on to that hope. Don't ever let it go. It will see you through.

*Be kind to you. Look in a mirror & say aloud: *I forgive you. I am forgiven.**

27

1. Today, choose you.
2. Write a list of your mostly deeply held wants, passions, hopes, & dreams.
3. Write down *everything* you would like to have/be/do/say while you're still around.
4. Don't edit. Don't worry *at all* about how you'll be able to make any of that list happen.
5. Just write down everything your heart desires.

*Be kind to you. Look in a mirror & say aloud: *I forgive you. I am forgiven.******

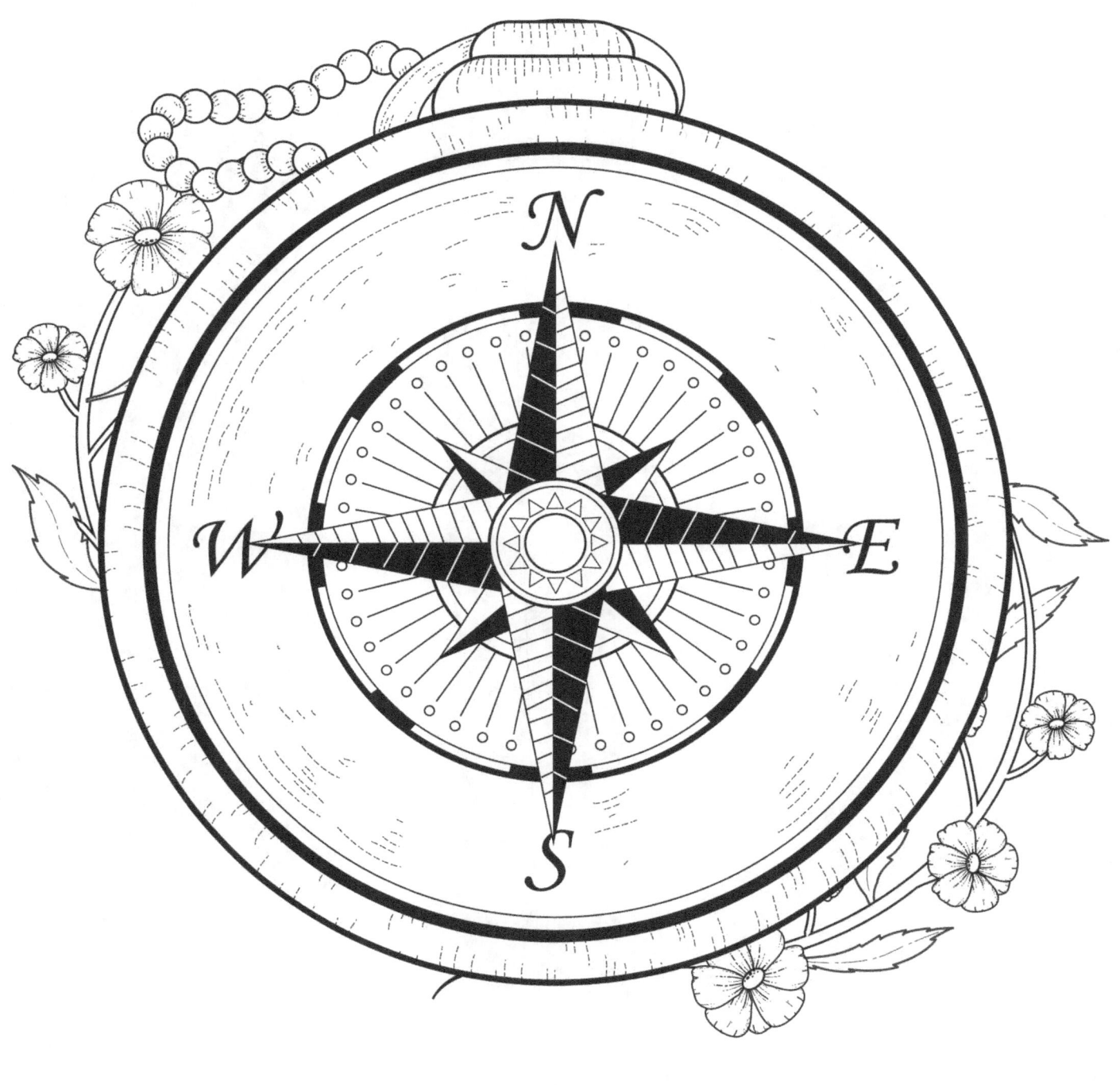

28

1. Today, move in the direction of your True North.
2. Read through your list from Day 27.
3. Now you know where your heart lies.
4. Keep that list as your focus. Read it aloud. Post it where you'll see it daily.
5. Throw all the positive energy you can at that list.
6. Now start moving in the direction that you most want to go & take at least one bold action today to make that list a reality. Repeat often.

*Be kind to you. Look in a mirror & say aloud: *I forgive you. I am forgiven.**

29

1. Today, love yourself.
2. Choose *daily* to love yourself enough to give yourself *unlimited* tries.
3. Choose *daily* to forgive yourself an *infinite* number of times.
4. Find peace.
5. Now look at your list from Day 8.
6. Pick one & do it today.
7. Then read through your list from Day 27.
8. Take another bold action today to make that list a reality. Repeat often.

Be kind to you. Look in a mirror & say aloud: *I forgive you. I am forgiven.*

30

1. Today, celebrate!
2. Be proud of yourself for how far you've come.
3. Write down your successes & victories (big or small).
4. Do something nice for yourself (like a prize for a job well done).
5. Go & enjoy your life!

Be kind to you. Look in a mirror & say aloud: I forgive you. I am forgiven.

ABOUT THE AUTHOR!

This book was born out of Shelli Johnson's own struggle to forgive herself. She wanted and needed to heal herself. She wanted and needed practical and easy steps she could take to make peace with herself so she could find joy in her life again. So she simply wrote the book she needed to read. Every day, she does her best to cut herself some slack & practice progress, not perfection.

Shelli's also an award-winning journalist (sports reporting), novelist (grand prize winner), and blogger (shellijohnson.com/blog). She's a truck owner, horse rider, photographer, yoga enthusiast, and slow-cooker fan (shellijohnson.com/recipes). Find out more at: shellijohnson.com/about

Find out about Shelli's other books at:
shellijohnson.com/books

GET YOUR FREE STUFF!

Visit: shellijohnson.com/signup
Opt-in for the newsletter to keep in touch.
Get a free bookmark to color.

ACKNOWLEDGMENTS!

My sincere thanks to people who make my days brighter:
Rollin Johnson
Heather Porazzo

Disclosures and Disclaimers

This book is published in print format. All trademarks and service marks are the properties of their respective owners. All references to these properties are made solely for editorial purposes. Except for marks actually owned by the Author or the Publisher, no commercial claims are made to their use, and neither the Author nor the Publisher is affiliated with such marks in any way.

Unless otherwise expressly noted, none of the individuals or business entities mentioned herein has endorsed the contents of this book.

Limits of Liability & Disclaimers of Warranties

Because this book is a general educational information product, it is not a substitute for professional advice on the topics discussed in it.

The materials in this book are provided "as is" and without warranties of any kind either express or implied. The Author and the Publisher disclaim all warranties, express or implied, including, but not limited to, implied warranties of merchantability and fitness for a particular purpose. The Author and the Publisher do not warrant that defects will be corrected. The Author does not warrant or make any representations regarding the use or the results of the use of the materials in this book in terms of their correctness, accuracy, reliability, or otherwise. Applicable law may not allow the exclusion of implied warranties, so the above exclusion may not apply to you.

Under no circumstances, including, but not limited to, negligence, shall the Author or the Publisher be liable for any special or consequential damages that result from the use of, or the inability to use this book, even if the Author, the Publisher, or an authorized representative has been advised of the possibility of such damages. Applicable law may not allow the limitation or exclusion of liability or incidental or consequential damages, so the above limitation or exclusion may not apply to you. In no event shall the Author or Publisher total liability to you for all damages, losses, and causes of action (whether in contract, tort, including but not limited to, negligence or otherwise) exceed the amount paid by you, if any, for this book.

You agree to hold the Author and the Publisher of this book, principals, agents, affiliates, and employees harmless from any and all liability for all claims for damages due to injuries, including attorney fees and costs, incurred by you or caused to third parties by you, arising out of the products, services, and activities discussed in this book, excepting only claims for gross negligence or intentional tort.

You agree that any and all claims for gross negligence or intentional tort shall be settled solely by confidential binding arbitration per the American Arbitration Association's commercial arbitration rules. Your claim cannot be aggregated with third party claims. All arbitration must occur in the municipality where the Author's principal place of business is located. Arbitration fees and costs shall be split equally, and you are solely responsible for your own lawyer fees.

Facts and information are believed to be accurate at the time they were placed in this book. All data provided in this book is to be used for information purposes only. The information contained within is not intended to provide specific legal, financial, tax, physical or mental health advice, or any other advice whatsoever, for any individual or company and should not be relied upon in that regard. The services described are only offered in jurisdictions where they may be legally offered. Information provided is not all-inclusive, and is limited to information that is made available and such information should not be relied upon as all-inclusive or accurate.

For more information about this policy, please contact the Author at the website address listed in the Copyright Notice at the front of this book.

IF YOU DO NOT AGREE WITH THESE TERMS AND EXPRESS CONDITIONS, DO NOT READ THIS BOOK. YOUR USE OF THIS BOOK, INCLUDING PRODUCTS, SERVICES, AND ANY PARTICIPATION IN ACTIVITIES MENTIONED IN THIS BOOK, MEAN THAT YOU ARE AGREEING TO BE LEGALLY BOUND BY THESE TERMS.

Affiliate Compensation & Material Connections Disclosure

This book may contain references to websites and information created and maintained by other individuals and organizations. The Author and the Publisher do not control or guarantee the accuracy, completeness, relevance, or timeliness of any information or privacy policies posted on these websites.

You should assume that all references to products and services in this book are made because material connections exist between the Author or Publisher and the providers of the mentioned products and services ("Provider"). You should also assume that all website links within this book are affiliate links for (a) the Author, (b) the Publisher, or (c) someone else who is an affiliate for the mentioned products and services (individually and collectively, the "Affiliate").

The Affiliate recommends products and services in this book based in part on a good faith belief that the purchase of such products or services will help readers in general.

The Affiliate has this good faith belief because (a) the Affiliate has tried the product or service mentioned prior to recommending it or (b) the Affiliate has researched the reputation of the Provider and has made the decision to recommend the Provider's products or services based on the Provider's history of providing these or other products or services.

The representations made by the Affiliate about products and services reflect the Affiliate's honest opinion based upon the facts known to the Affiliate at the time this book was published.

Because there is a material connection between the Affiliate and Providers of products or services mentioned in this book, you should always assume that the Affiliate may be biased because of the Affiliate's relationship with a Provider and/or because the Affiliate has received or will receive something of value from a Provider.

Perform your own due diligence before purchasing a product or service mentioned in this book.

The type of compensation received by the Affiliate may vary. In some instances, the Affiliate may receive complimentary products (such as a review copy), services, or money from a Provider prior to mentioning the Provider's products or services in this book.

In addition, the Affiliate may receive a monetary commission or non-monetary compensation when you take action by using a website link within in this book. This includes, but is not limited to, when you purchase a product or service from a Provider after going to a website link contained in this book.

Health Disclaimers

As an express condition to reading to this book, you understand and agree to the following terms.

This book is a general educational health-related information product. This book does not contain medical advice.

The book's content is not a substitute for direct, personal, professional medical care and diagnosis. None of the exercises or treatments (including products and services) mentioned in this book should be performed or otherwise used without prior approval from your physician or other qualified professional health care provider.

There may be risks associated with participating in activities or using products and services mentioned in this book for people in poor health or with pre-existing physical or mental health conditions.

Because these risks exist, you will not use such products or participate in such activities if you are in poor health or have a pre-existing mental or physical condition. If you choose to participate in these risks, you do so of your own free will and accord, knowingly and voluntarily assuming all risks associated with such activities.

Earnings & Income Disclaimers
No Earnings Projections, Promises or Representations
For purposes of these disclaimers, the term "Author" refers individually and collectively to the author of this book and to the affiliate (if any) whose affiliate hyperlinks are referenced in this book.

You recognize and agree that the Author and the Publisher have made no implications, warranties, promises, suggestions, projections, representations or guarantees whatsoever to you about future prospects or earnings, or that you will earn any money, with respect to your purchase of this book, and that the Author and the Publisher have not authorized any such projection, promise, or representation by others.

Any earnings or income statements, or any earnings or income examples, are only estimates of what you might earn. There is no assurance you will do as well as stated in any examples. If you rely upon any figures provided, you must accept the entire risk of not doing as well as the information provided. This applies whether the earnings or income examples are monetary in nature or pertain to advertising credits which may be earned (whether such credits are convertible to cash or not).

There is no assurance that any prior successes or past results as to earnings or income (whether monetary or advertising credits, whether convertible to cash or not) will apply, nor can any prior successes be used, as an indication of your future success or results from any of the information, content, or strategies. Any and all claims or representations as to income or earnings (whether monetary or advertising credits, whether convertible to cash or not) are not to be considered as "average earnings".

Testimonials & Examples
Testimonials and examples in this book are exceptional results, do not reflect the typical purchaser's experience, do not apply to the average person and are not intended to represent or guarantee that anyone will achieve the same or similar results. Where specific income or earnings (whether monetary or advertising credits, whether convertible to cash or not), figures are used and attributed to a specific individual or business, that individual or business has earned that amount. There is no assurance that you will do as well using the same information or strategies. If you rely on the specific income or earnings figures used, you must accept all the risk of not doing as well. The described experiences are atypical. Your financial results are likely to differ from those described in the testimonials.

The Economy
The economy, where you do business, on a national and even worldwide scale, creates additional uncertainty and economic risk. An economic recession or depression might negatively affect your results.

Your Success or Lack of It
Your success in using the information or strategies provided in this book depends on a variety of factors. The Author and the Publisher have no way of knowing how well you will do because they do not know you, your background, your work ethic, your dedication, your motivation, your desire, or your business skills or practices. Therefore, neither the Author nor the Publisher guarantees or implies that you will get rich, that you will do as well, or that you will have any earnings (whether monetary or advertising credits, whether convertible to cash or not), at all.

Businesses and earnings derived therefrom involve unknown risks and are not suitable for everyone. You may not rely on any information presented in this book or otherwise provided by the Author or the Publisher, unless you do so with the knowledge and understanding that you can experience significant losses (including, but not limited to, the loss of any monies paid to purchase this book and/or any monies spent setting up, operating, and/or marketing your business activities, and further, that you may have no earnings at all (whether monetary or advertising credits, whether convertible to cash or not).

Forward-Looking Statements
Materials in this book may contain information that includes or is based upon forward-looking statements within the meaning of the Securities Litigation Reform Act of 1995. Forward-looking statements give the Author's expectations or forecasts of future events. You can identify these statements by the fact that they do not relate strictly to historical or current facts. They use words such as "anticipate," "estimate," "expect," "project," "intend," "plan," "believe," and other words and terms of similar meaning in connection with a description of potential earnings or financial performance.

Any and all forward looking statements here or on any materials in this book are intended to express an opinion of earnings potential. Many factors will be important in determining your actual results and no guarantees are made that you will achieve results similar to the Author or anybody else. In fact, no guarantees are made that you will achieve any results from applying the Author's ideas, strategies, and tactics found in this book.

Purchase Price
Although the Publisher believes the price is fair for the value that you receive, you understand and agree that the purchase price for this book has been arbitrarily set by the Publisher or the vendor who sold you this book. This price bears no relationship to objective standards.

Due Diligence
You are advised to do your own due diligence when it comes to making any decisions. Use caution and seek the advice of qualified professionals before acting upon the contents of this book or any other information. You shall not consider any examples, documents, or other content in this book or otherwise provided by the Author or Publisher to be the equivalent of professional advice.

The Author and the Publisher assume no responsibility for any losses or damages resulting from your use of any link, information, or opportunity contained in this book or within any other information disclosed by the Author or the Publisher in any form whatsoever.

YOU SHOULD ALWAYS CONDUCT YOUR OWN INVESTIGATION (PERFORM DUE DILIGENCE)
BEFORE BUYING PRODUCTS OR SERVICES FROM ANYONE. THIS INCLUDES PRODUCTS AND SERVICES
SOLD VIA WEBSITE LINKS REFERENCED IN THIS BOOK.

www.ingramcontent.com/pod-product-compliance
Lightning Source LLC
Chambersburg PA
CBHW060515300426
44112CB00017B/2682